Yet another continent of life
remains to be discovered, not
upon the earth, but one two
hundred feet above it, extending
over thousands of square miles....
There awaits a rich
harvest for the
naturalist who
overcomes the obstacles —
gravitation, ants, thorns,
rotten trunks —
and mounts to the summits
of the jungle trees.

William Beebe
from *Tropical Wild Life*, 1917

Library of Congress Cataloging-in-Publication Data.
Liptak, Karen. Inside Biosphere 2: the rainforest / Karen Liptak. p. cm.
Includes bibliographical references (p.63) ISBN 1-882428-06-4 (pbk.) : $8.95
1. Rain forest ecology—Juvenile literature. 2. Rain forests—Juvenile literature.
3. Biosphere 2 (Project)—Juvenile literature. [1. Rain forest ecology. 2. Ecology.
3. Rain forests. 4. Biosphere 2 (Project)] I. Title. II. Title: Inside Biosphere Two.
QH541.5.R27L56 1993 574.5'2642'0913—dc20 93-21374

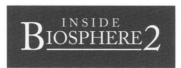

INSIDE
BIOSPHERE 2

The Rainforest

Karen Liptak

THE BIOSPHERE PRESS / Oracle, Arizona

SCARAB
BEETLE

LEOPARD
FROG

SOFT-SHELLED
TURTLE

COCONUT
PALM

THE BREATHTAKING STRUCTURE OF BIOSPHERE 2

On Sept. 26, 1991, the eyes of the world were focused on the southwestern corner of the United States. At the break of dawn, eight men and women stepped inside an extraordinary glass and steel structure and locked its door behind them. For the next two years their home would be a giant laboratory, sealed off from the rest of our planet.

VANILLA
PLANT

They were about to make history as the first crew of biospherians inside Biosphere 2, the experiment that gets its name because it's a miniature version of Biosphere 1, better known as Earth. The crew's mission was to study the 3,800 species of plants and animals and countless microbes also locked inside. It is a

...SPRAWLS BENEATH THE ARIZONA SUN.

STAGHORN CORAL

unique laboratory unlike any other ever built, created to replicate in miniature the way our planet works.

From a distance, the Biosphere 2 structure resembles a huge greenhouse, yet it is far more complex than any ordinary greenhouse. Inside it there are replicas of five separate tropical zones: a rainforest, a savannah, a desert, a marsh, and an ocean. Their atmosphere, soil, rock, and water are all a part of their own

THE FIRST CREW TO
LIVE IN BIOSPHERE 2

ROOSTER

BUTTERFLY FISH

BUTTERFLY

GALAGO

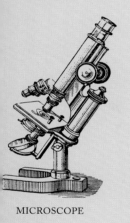

MICROSCOPE

self-sustaining world. Nothing but sunlight, sound, electricity, and scientific samples can pass through its walls of glass and steel. Biosphere 2 also has a human **habitat,** with living and working areas for the crew, and a farm in which they grow all their own food.

No one has ever done anything quite like this before, so isolated from the rest of the world. By investigating the delicate balance of the forces that sustain and support life inside Biosphere 2, scientists hope to find ways to manage and preserve Earth's environment. They also hope to learn how we can build future biospheres elsewhere on Earth, as well as on the Moon, Mars, and beyond. Some of the answers they seek are sure to be found in that marvel of **diversity:** the rainforest.

Words in **boldface** appear in the Glossary at the back of this book.

PART I:
THE OTHER CONTINENT

STEP INTO AN EMERALD WORLD

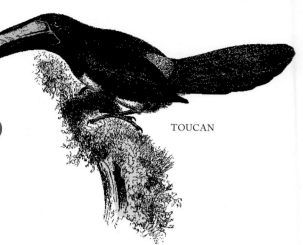

TOUCAN

Tropical rainforests are surely among the most beautiful mysteries of our planet. Richly endowed with wet, lush vegetation, they form a 'green belt' within a 3,000-mile-wide band along Earth's **Equator,** a geographic zone known as the **tropics.** For a long time modern-day people didn't pay too much attention to the rainforest — indeed, they didn't even know much about them! Then about a hundred and fifty years ago, explorers and scientists began to investigate them. Now we know that, among many other important things, tropical rainforests are the homes of the greatest diversity of plants and animals on Earth.

Although rainforests cover less than 7 percent of our planet's surface, they contain more than half of our plant and animal species. One scientist identified 450 tree species in only 2½

acres of rainforest in South America. By contrast, there are about 700 species of trees in the entire United States and Canada! But plants or trees aren't the only living things that thrive in the rainforests. For thousands of years, many animals and even people have also lived in harmony within these natural hothouses.

Rainforests owe their year-round parade of fruits, fragrant flowers, dazzling green leaves, and abundant seeds to a steady supply of sunlight and rain. The location of tropical rainforests within the equatorial belt, where the sun's position in the sky remains fairly constant all year long, grants them an endless summer with little change in their warm temperatures. And, of course, there is the rainfall for which rainforests get their name. Although some areas of rainforest may have occasional dry spells, they are usually drenched by over a hundred inches of rain a year. In most rainforests rain normally falls every two days out of three.

Just because a tropical forest receives a

THE BRANCHES OF A
CECROPIA REACH
TOWARD THOSE OF A
TREE FERN.

lot of rain doesn't mean it's a rainforest, however. The forest of Cherrapunji, India, receives a total of up to 460 inches of rain a year! But four months out of the year are completely dry, making it a 'seasonal jungle' rather than a rainforest.

If you were to load your backpack, put on a pith helmet, and step into a rainforest, you would enter a world probably quite unlike the usual notions we have of 'jungles'. For one thing, the silence — except for the chirping of katydids — would probably surprise you. Where is the cawing, hooting, squawking, and singing of all the birds you expected to hear? Even butterflies seem to flutter by in silence, without so much as stirring a breeze with their wings. You might also be surprised to find that plants are relatively sparse at the ground level, nowhere near the impenetrable wall of greenery you may have imagined!

Fascinating Facts

Average daytime temperature:

Between 70° and 80°F. Varies little

day by day.

Average rainfall: 72 to over 360

inches of rain a year.

Location: Extends approximately

10 degrees north and 10 degrees

south of the Equator.

Percent of Earth's total biomass:

As of 1993, approximately 7 percent

and shrinking every day.

Relative humidity: 100 percent at

night to less than 30 percent at noon.

9

Chances are, you would still know you were in a rainforest by the damp smell and the fragrance of flowers that fill the air, the moisture that makes your clothes sticky, and the many flying insects that make you glad you remembered your insect repellent. But most of all, there is the constant wetness. Even if it hasn't rained for hours, drops of water are always falling to the ground. Those that land on leaves glitter like jewels wherever the sunlight hits them. Yet the vegetation is so dense on top that even if you hear the booming thunderclap of a sudden

Rainforests Around the World

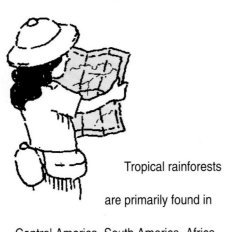

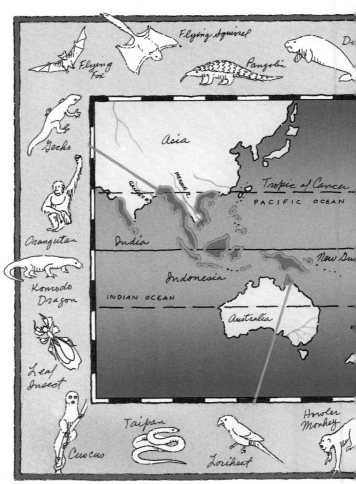

Tropical rainforests are primarily found in Central America, South America, Africa (chiefly in West Africa and Madagascar), and the southern regions of Asia. Australia has only a small area of rainforest left. Pacific islands within the tropical zone may also support extensive rainforests, such as the islands of New Guinea and Hawaii. The rainforest on Puerto Rico in the Caribbean Sea was used as a major collecting site for many Biosphere 2 rainforest plants.

downpour, it may take a good ten minutes before the drops filter through to reach you. (Strangely enough, rainforest rain feels cool to the skin, not warm.)

Perhaps you would feel a sense of mystery, even danger, as if something lurks unseen among the leaves. You would be right, for most of the rainforest's activity is hidden from your view. But if you look up, way up in the trees, you get a good idea of where most of the rainforest's action is.

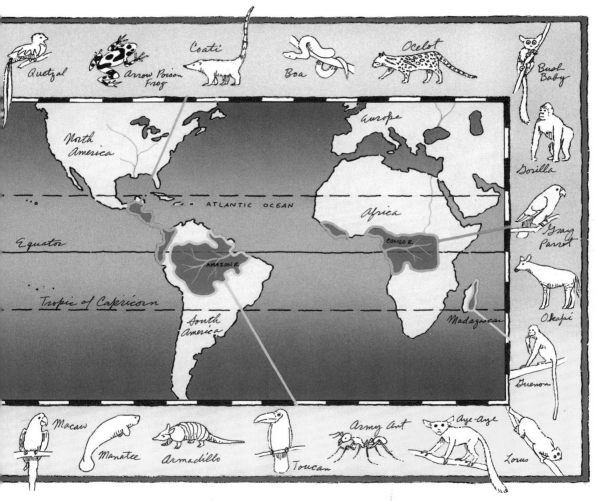

There are also **temperate** rainforests in areas that are cool, but not freezing. These can be found along the northwest coast of North America, in Canada and Alaska. While temperate rainforests are rich in life, they do not contain the abundance of species that tropical rainforests do.

HARPY
EAGLE

VIEW AT THE TOP

The unique character of each rainforest makes it a one-of-a-kind environment, with its own community of plants, animals, and tiny living things known as **microorganisms**. Yet all rainforests have much in common, including their basic three-story construction.

The thick green and leafy crown of trees in the top story, known as the **canopy**, caps the rainforest like a roof. Canopy trees, which may range from 75 to 150 feet above the forest floor, are usually very close together. The branches of these tall trees begin far from the ground near their tops. Flowers sometimes grow right on the trunks, rather than on their branches. The leaves at such heights are often small and waxy to keep water from evaporating, since the heat from direct sunlight is so intense in the tropics.

In some rainforests, the tallest trees poke through the canopy's flat, sun-drenched surface in scattered places. These giants, which may tower to heights of 200 feet or more, are called **emergents** (ee-MUR-jents). (Some people consider this a fourth story in the rainforest.) Many birds are at home here, including the harpy eagle, the largest eagle in the world. Found from Mexico to the Amazon, it feeds primarily on other birds, as well as on monkeys and sloths. Other birds at this level include woodpeckers and toucans (TOO-kons). Toucans have a boldly colored beak that is almost half their total body weight. Like many other emergent birds, toucans help some rainforest trees grow by dispersing seeds in their droppings while in flight. Many high-flying butterflies also live here, such as the beautiful metallic-hued blue morphos.

From below, your only hint of the activity in the canopy might be the partly

eaten fruits, cracked nuts, and broken twigs that come raining down around you. But scientists can tell you that some of the world's most fascinating plants and animals live or travel through here. Because the canopy's thin twigs and branches won't support the weight of large animals, those that live in the high branches are usually small. In South America, they include opossums, sloths, and a variety of monkeys.

Rainforest canopies around the world also hold a wealth of birds. In American jungles you will find both tiny hummingbirds and large parrots.

A BEAUTIFUL BROMELIAD IN THE
PUERTO RICAN RAINFOREST

Hummingbirds — the smallest birds yet discovered — have slender bills designed for reaching the sweet nectar in flowers, while parrots have large, strong bills that are ideal for cracking nuts. In Asia and Africa, you can find hornbills in the canopy level, too. Their enormous boldly colored beaks look deceptively heavy, but are actually a honeycomb of light-weight bony tissue in a protective shell of horn. If you could fly above the canopy and peer down with a powerful pair of binoculars,

THE PUERTO RICAN RAINFOREST IS DRENCHED IN SUNLIGHT. HUMIDITY IN THE AIR MAKES IT APPEAR HAZY.

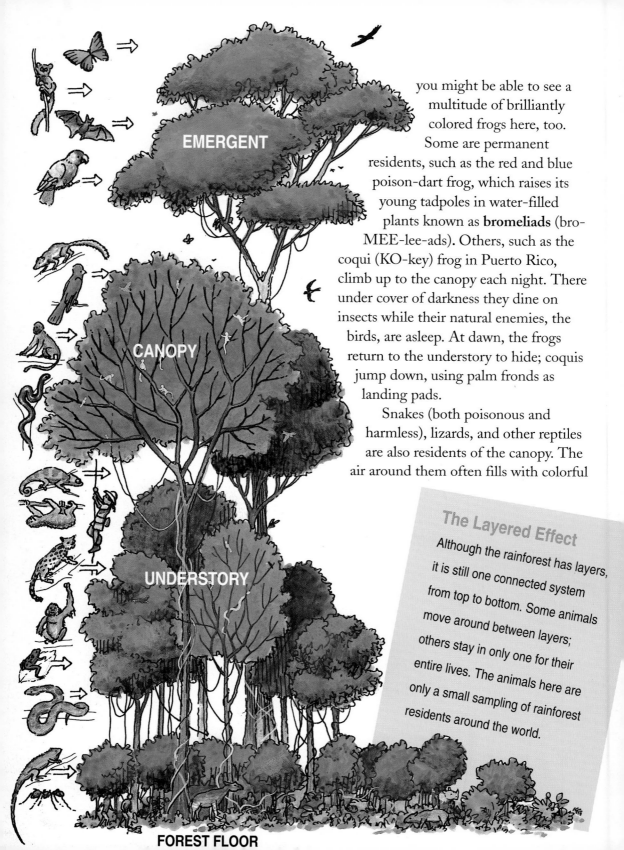

EMERGENT

CANOPY

UNDERSTORY

FOREST FLOOR

you might be able to see a multitude of brilliantly colored frogs here, too. Some are permanent residents, such as the red and blue poison-dart frog, which raises its young tadpoles in water-filled plants known as **bromeliads** (bro-MEE-lee-ads). Others, such as the coqui (KO-key) frog in Puerto Rico, climb up to the canopy each night. There under cover of darkness they dine on insects while their natural enemies, the birds, are asleep. At dawn, the frogs return to the understory to hide; coquis jump down, using palm fronds as landing pads.

Snakes (both poisonous and harmless), lizards, and other reptiles are also residents of the canopy. The air around them often fills with colorful

The Layered Effect

Although the rainforest has layers, it is still one connected system from top to bottom. Some animals move around between layers; others stay in only one for their entire lives. The animals here are only a small sampling of rainforest residents around the world.

The Slow and
Steady Sloths

butterflies, some as large as small birds. Should you reach this lofty layer you would surely discover countless other insects as well. These are the most numerous creatures in the canopy — and in the rainforest as a whole. Some are exotically colored, like the beautiful golden beetles of Costa Rica, which look like they're made of gold.

Other insects of the rainforest are sometimes deadly, such as the mosquitoes that cause malaria (ma-LAIR-ee-ah) and yellow fever. The tse-tse (a sharp slurring sound with a long 'ee') fly of Central Africa isn't too popular either: it causes the fatal 'sleeping sickness'. And the bite of a white fly in South America can infect its victim with leishmaniasis (LESH-ma-NI-ah-sis), a disease that eats away the cartilage under the face. Most insects are not restricted to one level of the rainforest, but can fly or crawl freely from canopy to floor. Many are giants among their kind; eight-inch millipedes and five-inch cockroaches are not rare. A mosquito net over your sleeping bag, anti-malaria pills, and other preventive measures are essential when exploring a rainforest!

Among the canopy plants, epiphytes (EP-uh-fights) grow rapidly at this level, their roots clutching other plants for support. However, like insects, **epiphytes** can be found in all layers of the rainforest, from the sunny canopy to the dark forest floor. Commonly known as 'air plants', they have no underground roots to touch

Sloths are so well adapted to canopy living that they are extremely clumsy on the ground. They spend most of their time hanging upside down from branches. Sloths seem very lazy, since everything they do is in slow motion, but to a sloth that is its normal way of life. In fact, it may take a full month for a sloth to digest a single meal, which may consist of the leaves, fruit, and buds of the cecropia tree. Dew is its only drink. Three-toed sloths of South America usually come down to the ground only once a week to defecate!

Green **algae** (AL-gee) growing on their fur helps the sloth hide from the harpy eagle and other predators. The fur also provides a home for several different types of insects. One of them, the sloth moth, lays its eggs in the sloth's fur. When the moth larvae hatch, they feed exclusively on the algae on the sloth's hair.

the soil. Instead, they use their roots only to grip onto other plants. Epiphytes take their water and food directly from the air. Many epiphytes are mosses, **lichens, orchids** (as many as forty species per tree!), and ferns. The bromeliads are especially important epiphytes because they provide places for animals to hide and breed.

Vines, including the woody lianas (lee-ANN-ahs), abound in the canopy. Lacking their own trunks for support, lianas wrap around tree trunks and branches to hitch a ride to the sky.

When they reach the canopy, these piggyback travelers may spread out among several trees, as if assigned by nature to hold the rainforest together. Although enchanting to see, lianas can be dangerous as well. A tree that falls can drag down others bound to it by the vines.

Another natural danger to rainforest trees comes from the strangler fig. The roots of the strangler fig grow around the trunk of a host tree and gradually kill it. In Southeast Asia, one type of strangler, the banyan tree, grows to enormous size and often becomes the center of village life in rural areas.

A TANGLE OF LIANAS ENTWINE
A TREE IN THE GLOOM OF A
RAINFOREST IN FRENCH GUIANA.

A HUGE STRANGLER FIG DWARFS
THE SURROUNDING TREES.

ENTER THE TWILIGHT ZONE

Below the bustling canopy level is a kind of twilight zone, sheltered from the intense sunlight by the thick canopy. Everywhere you look are trees — and more trees. Flecks of sunlight dapple the leaves of epiphytes and saplings, but aside from the river banks or clearings, dimness pervades. This is the **understory**, where plants that thrive in the shade do well. Some understory trees are already full-grown, like the oil palms whose fruit produces a useful cooking oil. Other trees are merely passing through the understory, destined to reach the canopy by the time they mature.

The largest number of bats in the world live in the tropics, where the understory suits them just fine. Like many other understory animals, these fascinating creatures are **nocturnal** and prefer its low-light environment. Most bats eat insects that fly at night. Others feed on fruit or nectar, and still others are **carnivores**, or meat-eaters. There are also vampire bats that feed on blood, usually from large grazing animals. Some scientists consider fruit- and nectar-eating bats to be the most important pollinators and seed-dispersing animals in the tropics. They help to spread **pollen** (the yellowish powder that contains the male reproductive cells of a plant) and seeds as they go about their daily lives; in fact, they eat the seeds and then expel them as waste as they fly. We owe our thanks to bats for such plants as bananas, peaches, mangos, figs, avocados, and cashews. They pollinate them all!

Bats are also important in re-seeding patches of tropical forest that have been cleared. They carry the seeds of the hardy trees and shrubs that start new growth in these areas. When the pioneer plants get large enough, they attract small mammals and birds. These animals in turn bring other kinds of seeds that add to the regrowth of the forest.

In American rainforests, the understory may also harbor the jaguar (JAG-wahr), the largest cat in the western hemisphere. Its orangish coat with black spots makes an excellent camouflage as it silently lurks

Those Great Apes

GORILLA

CHIMPANZEE

Primates, the group of mammals that includes human beings and others that most resemble them, is divided into two main types. One type includes tarsiers (TAR-see-ers), aye-ayes, galagos, and others. The other type consists of humans, apes, and monkeys.

There are four main types of apes. Except for gibbons, three (gorillas, chimpanzees, and orangutans) are considered 'the great apes'. None have tails and all live in the rainforests.

Gorillas, the largest apes, inhabit the rainforests of central Africa. Although powerful, they are quiet, peaceful animals that live in groups of two to thirty individuals. They're always on the move, usually traveling on the ground but climbing trees to find food and to sleep. Although gorillas are considered highly intelligent, chimpanzees are said to most resemble humans.

Chimpanzees are found in the tropical rainforests and the grassy plains of Africa. They live in groups that frequently change in size and members. They usually divide their time somewhat equally between ground and tree living, although they sleep in the trees each night.

Whereas most apes live with their families, orangutans (uh-RAN-ghu-tans) are rather solitary creatures. Their home is the dense rainforests of Southeast Asia. The male lives alone except during the breeding season. Females will stay with their young until the offspring can be on their own, usually at about five years old.

in the branches, ready to drop down onto the back of an unsuspecting deer or tapir below. Solitary and nocturnal, the magnificent jaguar pursues its prey just as readily in the treetops as on the ground. Known as "el tigre" throughout Latin America, it once ranged from the southern United States to northern Argentina.

Meat-eating cats within the African understory include palm civets and golden cats. Contrary to popular folklore, the African lion is not king of the jungle, for it much prefers the savannahs to the tropical rainforests. In Asia, the tiger is the large 'top cat' at the apex of the tropical **food web**. This beautiful carnivore actually originated in Siberia and then expanded its range into southern Asia as far as the islands of Indonesia. Now it is almost extinct in its birthplace. Although threatened in South Asia, preservation of their habitats by the

JAGUARS ARE FOND OF SPOTS LIKE THESE NEAR STREAMS.

government of India and conservation groups has helped to protect the tiger and other endangered rainforest species, such as the Indian rhinoceros. The Javan rhino and Sumatran rhino, who once roamed most of the rainforests of Southeast Asia, have been hunted almost to extinction.

Large snakes, including boa constrictors and anacondas, may stretch out on the branches of the South American rainforest's understory and wait for their prey: lizards, birds, even monkeys, and sometimes deer. Then they often climb up to the canopy or down to the ground level to find a quiet place to digest their meal and sun themselves.

THE ANACONDA CAN GROW TO THIRTY-EIGHT FEET LONG.

THE
FOREST FLOOR

If you want to see the world's masters of **decomposition**, focus on the thin carpet of leaf litter (dead leaves and twigs) on the rainforest floor. A good magnifying glass will probably reveal a myriad of insects, including termites, earthworms, and cockroaches, as well as **bacteria** and **fungi** (FUN-ji) — all of which carry out important daily chores in this often sunless part of the forest factory. Day after day they break down dead organic matter and recycle it into nutrients for living plants. In rainforests, litter decomposes 60 times faster than in temperate forests.

Surprisingly, the soil of the forest floor is very poor in the food materials that plants eat. Ninety percent of the tropical rainforest's nutrients are in its plants, rather than in the soil.

You will see some of nature's most exotically camouflaged insects here, such as the leaf butterfly which can look just like a dead leaf dangling on a branch or the striking flower mantis which has been mistaken for a beautiful white blossom. There are also numerous species of ants at this level. The small, ferocious army ants may travel in columns of as many as 20 million ants and eat any animals in their path, even wounded elephants! Some people of the rainforest welcome the arrival of army ants into their homes, because the ants eat all unwanted insects before moving on through the forest.

The forest floor is also home to big animals. In both the

A SNAIL LEISURELY MUNCHES ON RAINFOREST DEBRIS.

GIANT
ANTEATER

Amazon and the Southeast Asian rainforest, these include the tapirs who spend much of their time in jungle rivers. White-lipped peccaries and deer also live in South America, as does that toothless wonder of the animal world, the anteater. Anteaters use their giant claws to rip open termite nests, then lick up the termites with a two-foot-long tongue! Another South American rainforest inhabitant with a long, sticky tongue and a taste for termites is the armadillo, whose body is protected by a movable 'suit of armor' and whose keen sense of smell makes up for its poor eyesight.

Another famous, large, rainforest carnivore in Asia is the terrible komodo (ko-MO-do) dragon of Indonesia. This 10-foot-long giant lizard was considered a mere myth until biologists verified its existence in 1912. It eats both small and

A PATCH OF FUNGI SPROUTS FROM
THE FOREST FLOOR.

HUNGRY ANTS ATTACK AN UNLUCKY
TERMITE COLONY.

Decomposition:

Breaking down something into its component parts.

large animals and has been seen swimming in the open sea between islands!

On the ground level in African rainforests you may find elephants, gorillas, and okapis (oh-KAH-pees, giraffe-like creatures that were first discovered by scientists in the twentieth century). The largest rainforest animal in Southeast Asia is the rhinoceros.

In this dark forest zone, plants often have leaves with special 'drip tip' shapes that allow rainwater to drop off quickly. This keeps the water from blocking out the less than 2 percent of sunlight that manages to reach the floor of the rainforest.

Gaps in the forest canopy sometimes allow sunlight to flood the understory level and the forest floor. Then vegetation explodes with all kinds of growth! These clearings are often created by violent weather conditions, as when wind or lightning topples trees or breaks large branches. Gaps also result when trees keel over because their roots are too shallow to anchor them to the rainforest's thin soil during heavy rainfall. People also create gaps when they clear rainforest areas for gardening. Native groups used to thin out trees from small areas in the Amazon rainforest to plant their vegetables. After harvesting their crops, they would move on to another part of the forest. Whatever the cause, within a few years, the three levels of rainforest again cover the clearings.

A TREE EXPOSED TO SUNLIGHT SPORTS A BEARDLIKE GROWTH OF EPIPHYTES.

The Tropical Cafeteria

A complex cycle of food, food-eaters, and waste matter makes up the **food web**, in which energy and nutrients are passed from one organism to another.

Plants supply food for plant-eaters, or **herbivores** — a large group of animals ranging from elephants and gorillas to bees and other bugs. In turn, most herbivores are food for the meat-eating animals, or **carnivores**. At the top of the food web in many rainforests is a carnivore, such as the jaguar in the Amazon or the tiger in India. Some animals, including the galago of Africa, eat both plants and animals. These are **omnivores**, as are human beings.

All animals and plants produce waste and eventually die. Some large animals eat other animals that have died, but most of the waste—including dead plants and animals — becomes food for small **detritivores.** Billions of insects, worms, and centipedes, as well as fungi, tiny microbes, and other soil and water dwellers process billions of tons of once-living matter every year. Minerals, chemical elements, and water are all recycled nutrients that feed the plants and begin the food cycle once again.

KOMODO DRAGON

TIGER

23

PIECING TOGETHER THE JUNGLE JIGSAW

In the incredibly complex and beautiful world of the rainforest, each creature and plant has a special role to fill. Wherever you look, there are wonderful examples of species interaction. These include certain ants that make their nests in the roots of epiphytes. In turn, the bits of plant matter and soil they carry to their nests serve as food for the epiphytes. Then there are the Azteca ants that eat tiny growths on the fragile cecropia (seh-CROW-pee-ah) tree and live in its hollow stems. The ants eat any epiphytes that try to grow on the cecropia, keeping the tree free from heavy plants that could break its delicate limbs.

The pollinators are another example of cooperation. Pollen is transferred in the rainforest by bats, insects, and birds. Many of these rainforest go-betweens can only pollinate one type of plant, and many plants can only be pollinated by one type of animal. For example, the showy orchis, a kind of orchid, can be pollinated only by female bumblebees. The specialization in the rainforest is a curse at times, since destruction of even one part of it can totally wipe out whole species of plants or animals forever.

A HELICONIA FLOWER

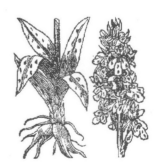

THE ORCHIS FLOWER

AN AGOUTI AND A
BRAZIL NUT

An interesting example of this specialization is the jungle triangle formed by the brazil nut, the bee, and the small rodent called the agouti (ah-GOO-tee). Brazil nuts come from a 150-foot-tall tree that grows in South America. However, these tasty nuts are dependent upon an interesting arrangement with both bees and agoutis. First the bees pollinate the brazil-nut flowers. Then the agoutis, the only animals that can crack open the hard shells around the nuts, eat the 'meat' inside. Later, the agouti eliminates the seeds, which take root in the soil and produce more Brazil nut trees.

A KING VULTURE LOOKS OVER THE REMAINS OF A PECCARY SKULL.

Where Rubber Bands Come From

The natural rubber found in such common items as rubber bands and bicycle tires comes from a milky white liquid called **latex**. This sticky sap runs just beneath the bark of rubber trees, which are native to the Amazon. Latex is collected by rubber tappers who make a cut in the bark and let the sap run into a bucket. In the nineteenth century, when people first discovered how to process rubber and use it, people flocked to the Amazon Basin to get in on the rubber boom. Later, European businessmen took seeds to Southeast Asia, and new rubber plantations sprang up in Malaysia, Vietnam, and elsewhere. Today Brazil produces only 1 percent of the world's rubber and must import some to satisfy its own needs! Brazilian rubber tappers are among the leaders in the fight to preserve the rainforest.

FROM THUNDERSTORMS TO CHOCOLATE

AFRICAN GRAY
PARROT

THE BUTTRESSED TRUNK OF A

The rainforest affects not only those species living in it, but also every other living thing on the planet. In Biosphere 1, rainforests are vital to the entire global balance of nature. There are several reasons for this.

Of course, the plants of the rainforest provide a food base for many animals, including humans. Yet the food connection is not our only link to the rainforest. It is also a major player in Earth's global environment, helping to determine what forms of life can exist here by its effect on atmospheric gases, including oxygen and carbon dioxide.

As the plants process sunlight during **photosynthesis** (FOE-toe-SIN-the-sis), oxygen is released into the air. All animals need this gas in the atmosphere to survive. If there were too little of it, most living things, including humans, would suffocate and die. (Too much oxygen is dangerous, too, since it can cause the spontaneous outbreak of fire.) Much of the oxygen in

Earth's atmosphere comes from microscopic plants living in the ocean, but rainforests with their abundant greenery are also prime producers of oxygen.

Its trees and other green plants also help to control the amount of carbon dioxide in the air. Carbon dioxide contributes to the **greenhouse effect** because it absorbs heat from the sun and keeps it from escaping into space, just like the glass in a greenhouse does. Plants absorb it during photosynthesis and use the carbon to make their food.

Some scientists are concerned that people are creating an alarming increase in carbon dioxide lately, because the burning

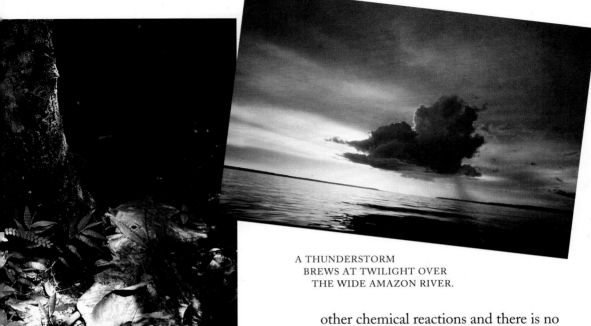

A THUNDERSTORM
BREWS AT TWILIGHT OVER
THE WIDE AMAZON RIVER.

TREE IS DAPPLED WITH SUNLIGHT.

other chemical reactions and there is no need for alarm. For now, scientists continue to study Earth's carbon cycle, hoping to understand it better.

Scientists also continue studying the effect rainforests have on Earth's weather systems. Weather reports on TV give you some idea of how rainforests thousands of miles away can affect our everyday life. Reporters often use weather maps of moving air masses to explain tomorrow's

of gas, coal, and oil releases carbon dioxide into the air. This uncontrolled burning could lead to a 'global warming' of rising temperatures worldwide. Everything could change, from rainfall and other weather conditions to where crops could grow. (Temperate zones, where most agriculture is, would shift farther away from the Equator than they are today.) A rise in temperature could also cause sea levels to rise as ice packs melt. This would lead to higher tides along the coasts. New York and London commuters might have to get to work by boat!

Other scientists say that the excess carbon dioxide is being controlled by

If I was a fairy godmother, the gift I would bestow on young naturalists would be a month in a tropical forest. It would alter their whole outlook on the incredible world we live in.

Gerald Durrell, *A Practical Guide for the Amateur Naturalist*

weather, be it a storm on its way up from the tropics or a cold wave moving down from the poles.

In Biosphere 1, tropical air heated by the sun rises and moves towards the North or South poles. The mass of air carries moisture with it, which helps to hold in the sun's energy as heat. Meanwhile, colder air from the poles is moving towards the Equator. This constant circulation of air is called **convection**. And wherever a mass of hot tropical air meets a mass of cool polar air, we get a narrow boundary known as a front. These hot and cold air masses at fronts are stirred into an atmospheric stew that brings changes in our weather, including thunderstorms.

Although the movement of air is a complicated subject, you can imagine what it is like if you picture a pot of water boiling on the stove. It has many bubbles in it which rise in the center, where the heat is most intense, and sink in other parts, where the pot is cooler. This is similar to the rising and sinking of Earth's hot and cold air masses. According to some scientists, the most critical feature of tropical air is the moisture it carries, because of its crucial role in the world's water cycle. And it's all those rainforest plants that help transfer water slowly and steadily into the atmosphere all year round.

The moisture is released through the

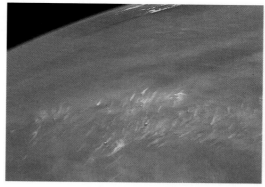

ASTRONAUTS IN THE SPACE SHUTTLE CAN SEE SMOKE PLUMES RISING FROM FIRES IN THE AMAZON RAINFOREST.

pores of plants in a process called **transpiration,** as well as in **evaporation** from the surfaces of leaves and from the soil. The moisture becomes water vapor, which turns into rain clouds as it cools or condenses. Some of it returns to the rainforest during the next rainfall; some of it joins the larger air masses and falls elsewhere. This continuous cycle of rain forming and falling is one of Earth's many amazing examples of recycling. And, most amazing, *the same water molecules* have gone through the water cycle again and again during Earth's entire history!

Scientists have found that land covered by trees stores and returns to the air at least ten times more moisture than land *without* vegetation and two times more than land covered with green plants other than trees. In other words, rainforests need their trees in order to continue making rain!

Plus rainforests act like giant sponges. They soak up the rainfall and gradually

Earth's Atmosphere: Blowing Hot and Cold

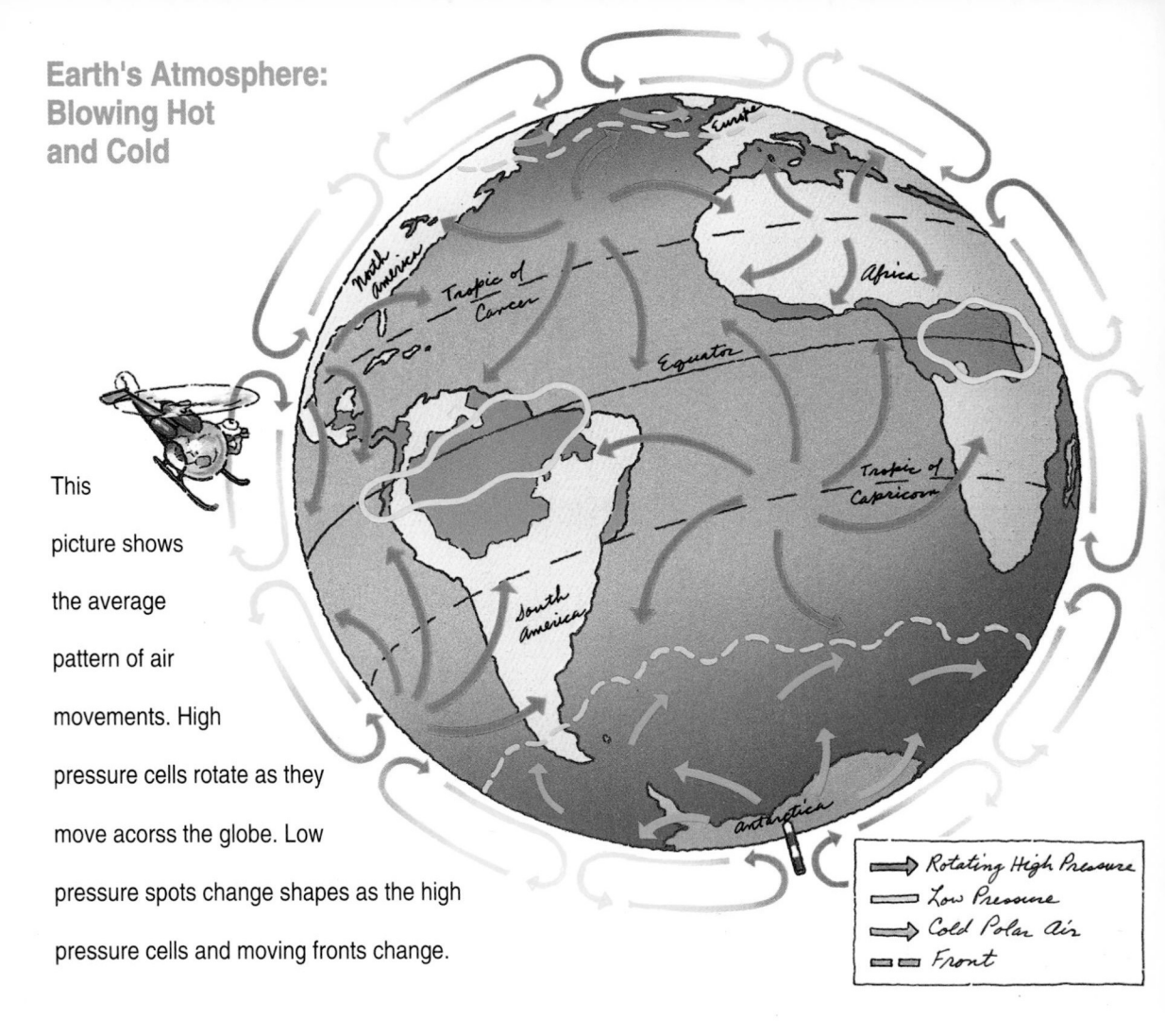

This picture shows the average pattern of air movements. High pressure cells rotate as they move acorss the globe. Low pressure spots change shapes as the high pressure cells and moving fronts change.

Rotating High Pressure
Low Pressure
Cold Polar Air
Front

release much of it into streams and rivers. In this way, they provide a constant supply of fresh water for people living even thousands of miles away. Eventually rivers flow into the ocean. The Amazon, for example, dumps a mind-boggling 56,107,438 gallons of fresh water into the Atlantic Ocean every second, eleven times more than the mighty Mississippi!

The Amazon River system also covers a larger area than any other river system in the world (2.3 million square miles). It extends from the Andes Mountains across South America to the Atlantic Ocean, a journey of about 4,000 miles. This 'king of rivers' is fed by over 1,000 smaller rivers and contains over 20 percent of the world's fresh water.

The Amazon's impact on the Atlantic Ocean is so powerful, in fact, that at 100

Native Amazonians have been using the Amazon as a means of transportation and a source of food for thousands of years. But Europeans didn't travel its length until 1542. A scouting party of sixty men led by Francisco de Orellaña was searching for food for their expedition when they were caught by the powerful current and carried into a river so large that it seemed to the Dominican friar Gaspar de Carvajal, who kept a journal of their ordeal, that they had "launched out upon a vast sea."

After many hardships, they made their way to Venezuela

A TRIBUTARY RIVER WINDS IT WAY THROUGH THE LUSH AMAZON RAINFOREST.

where they told strange tales of their experience. Carvajal reported being attacked by fierce, muscular women who fought with the skill of men. His report so struck his countrymen when it reached Spain that they named the river the Amazon, after the legendary warrior women of Greek myth.

Humans aren't the only ones that depend on the river for their existence. It supports over 5,000 different kinds of fish. Herons, egrets, and other birds fish along the river bank. You will also find the caiman here, a broad-snouted member of the alligator family. The largest of these carnivores is the black

A GROUP OF AMAZONIAN NATIVES AWAIT THE ARRIVAL OF VISITORS.

THE TRADITIONAL BONGO IS THE COMMON MEANS OF TRANSPORTATION.

caiman of the Amazon and lower Orinoco rivers, which can reach 15 feet (4.5 meters) long and is nearly extinct due to the demand for its skin. You may also find such mammals as tapirs and capybaras spending much of their time in the water.

The Amazon is also home to that endangered sea mammal known as the manatee or sea cow, a timid creature which can weigh as much as 3,000 pounds and was mistaken for the mythical mermaid by early explorers.

CAIMANS LAZE ALONG THE RIVER WHILE HERONS PREEN ABOVE.

CINCHONA

miles away from shore, you can still get a drink of fresh water. It is so vast and parts of it are so isolated that several of its tributary rivers have been discovered only recently through satellite scanning.

Atmosphere, water, and weather are part of the big picture. But they're not the only way that you are connected to tropical rainforests. Many of your favorite everyday foods come from rainforests. Cocoa and chocolate, avocados, bananas, oranges, and rice originate there. Coffee, vanilla, Brazil nuts, and a variety of spices also come from these tropical supermarkets. Many of our favorite species of houseplants, including African violets, bromeliads, and many decorative ferns, originate in the rainforest, as well.

The rainforests' greatest contributions to modern life, however, come from medicines derived from its plants. Today, one out of every four modern medicines is produced from rainforest plants. These have helped in the treatment of cancer (including childhood leukemia and Hodgkin's disease), high blood pressure,

and many other conditions. The treatment for malaria came from the mountain slopes above the rainforest — from the cinchona (chin-CONE-ah) plant, first collected by French physician and **botanist** Aime Bonpland in the early nineteenth century. If you ever swallow a poison, your doctor might recommend a medicine called ipecac (IP-eh-kak) to induce vomiting. Ipecac comes from a tree root found in the Amazon. Yet this is just the beginning. According to Dr. Michael Balick of the New York Botanical Gardens, less than 1/2 of 1 percent of flowering plants have been thoroughly studied to determine their full medicinal potential!

Our rainforests are vital for another excellent reason. They hold a stock of original **genes**. Genes are found in the cells of all living organisms and contain the instructions for making a copy of the organism itself. We all inherit our own genes from our parents. Without that information a species cannot reproduce. These genes may be needed in the future to help us 'restock' a threatened species. For instance, if a food crop we have discovered, cultivated, and come to depend upon is wiped out by a devastating disease or pest, then the original plant, still growing in the wild, could supply us with a replacement crop.

VALUABLE, YET VANISHING

If intelligent visitors from another planet were to see how much we have at stake in the rainforests, they would probably expect human beings to be very careful guardians of such a precious resource. Imagine how shocked they would be to learn that these treasures are being destroyed at a rapid rate.

In fact, experts estimate that the rainforests on our planet are vanishing at the rate of 50 to 100 acres per minute. That means that each year we lose enough rainforest to equal in size the state of Washington! As a result, many rainforest plants and animals have become **extinct.** More and more are becoming endangered. Yet those who study the rainforest realize that tucked away in some unexplored rainforest canopy there might be a plant that contains a cure for cancer, the common cold, or AIDS. Or a shrub that produces a new fruit to perk up family picnics or a new fiber to strengthen that family picnic basket.

Yanomami of the Amazon

People have lived and flourished in tropical rainforests for millennia. The Yanomami tribe, which numbers about 20,000, lives in the Amazon rainforest of Venezuela and Brazil. Yanomami villages usually consist of about seventy-five people, who share a big circular house. Although they hunt animals and gather wild plants, the mainstay of the Yanomami diet comes from their gardens.

Recently, public attention has been focused on the Yanomami because their lives and territory are being threatened, primarily by miners who want the rich mineral resources on their land.

Like other rainforest natives, the Yanomami live in harmony with the rainforest and rely on it for their existence. Scientists owe much of their present-day knowledge of the rainforest to natives who share what they know.

PAPAYA

February 29, [1832]: Delight...is a weak term to express the feelings of a naturalist who, for the first time, has wandered by himself in a Brazilian forest. The elegance of the grasses, the novelty of the parasitical plants, the beauty of the flowers, the glossy green of the foliage, but above all, the general luxuriance of the vegetation filled me with admiration. A most paradoxical mixture of sound and silence pervades the shady parts of the wood. The noise from the insects is so loud that it may be heard even in a vessel anchored several hundred yards from the shore; yet within the recesses of the forest a universal silence appears to reign....

Charles Darwin, *Journal of Researches into the Natural History and Geology of the Countries Visited During the Voyage Round the World of H.M.S. Beagle under the Command of Captain Fitzroy, R.N.*

The plight of our rainforests was no secret when Biosphere 2 was being planned. Botanist Ghillean Prance enthusiastically accepted the position as its rainforest design consultant. He suspected that the Biosphere 2 rainforest could serve many valuable purposes. For one thing, he saw it as a large-scale way to educate people about the important role rainforests play in preserving Earth's future and about our equally important role in preserving them. He also thought that the project could help us find out just how adaptable a rainforest is. Could you really build one and keep it going *in the middle of a North American desert?*

PART II:
RAINFOREST UNDER GLASS

A MINI RAINFOREST IN A MINI WORLD

Biosphere 2 is the result of the dreams and hard work of many designers, architects, engineers, environmentalists, as well as scientists specializing in many fields. They all share a strong desire to better understand and preserve our whole planet, rainforests and all.

Although many people didn't believe it could be done, gradually the 'impossible dream' of Biosphere 2 began to take shape. When designing its five wild zones, the planners of Biosphere 2 separated the rainforest and the desert as much as possible in order to keep the rainforest plants from invading the desert and the desert plants from invading the rainforest. Even so, the rainforest is only 300 feet away from the desert and only a staircase away from the Biosphere 2 ocean. If a biospherian working in the rainforest wants to cool off, he or she can walk down to the ocean in just two minutes!

WHITE'S TREEFROG

THE MAN-MADE MOUNTAIN DOMINATES THE RAINFOREST LANDSCAPE INSIDE BIOSPHERE 2.

The basic building block of Biosphere 2 is a very strong five-foot-long tube of steel called a spaceframe. Thousands of glass window panes — each weighing 250 pounds — are mounted on the frames. A stainless-steel bottom separates the main structure from the ground below. The glass and steel are sealed so tightly that virtually no air or moisture can pass through. It is the most tightly sealed building in the world — even more tightly sealed than the space shuttle!

Support facilities around Biosphere 2 include greenhouses, a Test Module, laboratories, and offices. There is also a Mission Control building, where the 'outside crew' uses technological equipment connected to a complex

Biosphere:
The domain of life, the part of the Earth in which life exists or which can support life, made up of many complex ecosystems.

It reaches from underground to way up in the atmosphere.

Biome: A distinct natural region where plants, animals, and other organisms live together under similar conditions of climate, terrain, and altitude. Biomes may be on land — such as rainforests or deserts — or in water — such as marshes or deep-water ocean.

Ecosystem: A community of living organisms and their environment that together form an inter-connected, interdependent whole.

Biology: The study of life.

Ecology: The branch of biology that studies the relationships of living things with each other and with their environment.

computer system to keep a constant watch over the Biosphere and its inhabitants.

There were many reasons to include a rainforest in Biosphere 2. Of course, the great diversity of life in rainforests gave the planners a wide choice of plants and animals to choose from as they decided what to include inside. They knew that the variety of species and **ecosystems** would provide more than pretty scenery. As on Earth itself, diversity helps Biosphere 2 do its job of maintaining life.

But exactly *how* each ecosystem helps the global biosphere is the big question. As Mark Nelson, a crew member during the first closure experiment, said, "What we don't know far exceeds what we do know. In reality, we don't know enough about the global biosphere to make very good predictions about it. So one of the things we want to study over the lifetime of Biosphere 2 is what the rainforest does for our biosphere."

Much of the research currently going on in Biosphere 2 concerns carbon dioxide. The rainforest is active all year in producing oxygen and recycling Biosphere 2's carbon dioxide. Two of the other biomes, the savannah and the desert, follow natural seasonal patterns and spend part of the year in a dormant state. This pattern of staggered activity in some biomes and constant activity in others was carefully orchestrated to help control the amount of carbon dioxide in the atmosphere. The scientists knew in advance that controlling carbon dioxide would be a challenge in a world so much smaller than our Earth.

In general terms, Biosphere 2 is especially important because it was built to last 100 years, so scientists will be able to study it over a long period of time. The project's planners also felt that Biosphere 2 provided an excellent way to study the workings of the rainforest as part of an entire biosphere. They hope that this information will someday provide new ideas for restoring damaged rainforests in Biosphere 1. They also hope that the knowledge gained will help us preserve Earth's remaining rainforests.

Part of Biosphere 2's rainforest is

THE CARBON DIOXIDE EFFLUX METER, AFFECTIONATELY KNOWN AS `R2D2,' MEASURES THE AMOUNT OF CARBON DIOXIDE IN THE BIOSPHERE 2 ATMOSPHERE.

38

A GROUP OF AMAZONIAN NATIVES AWAIT THE ARRIVAL OF VISITORS.

THE TRADITIONAL BONGO IS THE COMMON MEANS OF TRANSPORTATION.

caiman of the Amazon and lower Orinoco rivers, which can reach 15 feet (4.5 meters) long and is nearly extinct due to the demand for its skin. You may also find such mammals as tapirs and capybaras spending much of their time in the water. The Amazon is also home to that endangered sea mammal known as the manatee or sea cow, a timid creature which can weigh as much as 3,000 pounds and was mistaken for the mythical mermaid by early explorers.

CAIMANS LAZE ALONG THE RIVER WHILE HERONS PREEN ABOVE.

31

CINCHONA

miles away from shore, you can still get a drink of fresh water. It is so vast and parts of it are so isolated that several of its tributary rivers have been discovered only recently through satellite scanning.

Atmosphere, water, and weather are part of the big picture. But they're not the only way that you are connected to tropical rainforests. Many of your favorite everyday foods come from rainforests. Cocoa and chocolate, avocados, bananas, oranges, and rice originate there. Coffee, vanilla, Brazil nuts, and a variety of spices also come from these tropical supermarkets. Many of our favorite species of houseplants, including African violets, bromeliads, and many decorative ferns, originate in the rainforest, as well.

The rainforests' greatest contributions to modern life, however, come from medicines derived from its plants. Today, one out of every four modern medicines is produced from rainforest plants. These have helped in the treatment of cancer (including childhood leukemia and Hodgkin's disease), high blood pressure,

and many other conditions. The treatment for malaria came from the mountain slopes above the rainforest — from the cinchona (chin-CONE-ah) plant, first collected by French physician and **botanist** Aime Bonpland in the early nineteenth century. If you ever swallow a poison, your doctor might recommend a medicine called ipecac (IP-eh-kak) to induce vomiting. Ipecac comes from a tree root found in the Amazon. Yet this is just the beginning. According to Dr. Michael Balick of the New York Botanical Gardens, less than 1/2 of 1 percent of flowering plants have been thoroughly studied to determine their full medicinal potential!

Our rainforests are vital for another excellent reason. They hold a stock of original **genes.** Genes are found in the cells of all living organisms and contain the instructions for making a copy of the organism itself. We all inherit our own genes from our parents. Without that information a species cannot reproduce. These genes may be needed in the future to help us 'restock' a threatened species. For instance, if a food crop we have discovered, cultivated, and come to depend upon is wiped out by a devastating disease or pest, then the original plant, still growing in the wild, could supply us with a replacement crop.

THE CLOUD FOREST IN BIOSPHERE 2 IS HIDDEN BY A LAYER OF FOG.

LIMESTONE FORMATIONS SUCH AS THIS ONE IN VENEZUELA WERE THE MODELS FOR THE BIOSPHERE 2 MOUNTAIN.

ONE OF THE BEST WAYS TO SEE THE WHOLE PICTURE IS FROM THE AIR!

designed to be a cloud forest, high enough to get its water directly from the clouds. The highest point in Biosphere 2 is its ninety-foot ceiling, which towers above the rainforest's fifty-foot mountain. As you may imagine, building a rainforest mountain in Arizona took some special wizardry. Since moving a mountain to the site was impossible, it had to be created from scratch.

Using a real mountain in the Orinoco river valley of Venezuela as their guide, the makers of Biosphere 2 first built a skeleton out of steel rods. The skeleton was covered with several inches of concrete that was sprayed on and allowed to dry. Then another layer of concrete and sand was formed into the shape and texture of natural rock. Finally, the new 'mountain' was painted a natural-looking charcoal grey.

Pockets of soil in the sides of the artificial mountain hold tropical plants, so that it looks very much like a small mountain in the wild. But even if the outside of the mountain fooled you, the

TIGER POND WAS BUILT RIGHT
INTO THE SIDE OF THE
RAINFOREST MOUNTAIN.
AT LEFT, HOW IT APPEARED
UNDER CONSTRUCTION.

inside would not. It is a hollow chamber with storage area and a spiral staircase leading to the basement. The chamber serves as one of the major channels for circulating air throughout the rainforest. The air in Biosphere 2 is kept moving in a similar way to that on Earth: by natural convection. Because Biosphere 2 has a roof with varying heights, the air can rise and fall as in nature. Pumps draw the air from the high rainforest down through cooling coils in the basement. Then pumps and fans return the cooled air back to the lower desert.

The inside of the mountain also holds a misting machine, which creates the artificial fog high on top of the mountain. The health of the tropical plants depends in large part on the almost continual mist and the high humidity. But the rainforest needs more than frequent misting to survive. For that matter, water must be kept circulating throughout the entire structure. A computer-controlled system of pumps and overhead sprinklers does most of the job. Where necessary, manual action takes the place of programmed timers. This is a world where weather

reports have been replaced by 'weather requests'.

The top of the rainforest mountain holds a fresh water pond, which the biospherians call Little Tiger Pond. It feeds the waterfall cascading down the rocks into Tiger Pond which then empties into Crystal Creek, a stream that flows to the edge of the savannah. From there the water is pumped back up to the top of the mountain.

A RESEARCHER MAPS THE
PLANTS AND MAJOR FEATURES
OF BIOSPHERE 2.

Mapping Biosphere 2

All the wilderness biomes

of Biosphere 2 were surveyed by a team

of professionals before the structure was

sealed. The surveying information was

then fed into a computer program which

created maps of the 'geography' of the

Biosphere, complete with indications of

the first plantings. Then after the first

two-year experiment, the biomes were

surveyed again and compared with those

early maps. These maps are very

important because they

allow people to follow the

changes in each biome as

the experiments in

Biosphere 2 continue.

7,000 Tons of Soil and Flying Trees

A BULLDOZER SPREADS SOIL
INSIDE THE RAINFOREST.

Before plants could be installed inside this unique world, bedrock and soil had to be laid down. Originally, the planners wanted soil from a natural rainforest, but that would have been too impractical to transport or to sterilize. Perhaps soil from Arizona would do, they thought. Sonoran Desert soil was tested to see if it had the necessary microbes to perform the functions of litter decomposition, air filtering, mineral processing, and more. Sure, enough it did! So about 7,000 tons of desert soil were deposited to a depth of twelve to sixteen feet in order to accommodate full-grown trees.

Once the soil was in place, vegetation could follow. Before most of the plants went into the Biosphere, however, they were kept in quarantine greenhouses to make sure they had no harmful pests. Both the state of Arizona and the United States Department of Agriculture required the use of chemicals to kill any pests hiding in the plants. Here, too, was a challenge. Biosphere 2 researchers then had to develop safe ways to clean the plants of the poisons in some of the chemical sprays that the laws had required them to use!

Trees were planted first. Forklifts were recruited to transplant the trees — some

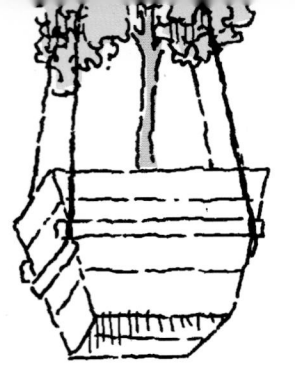

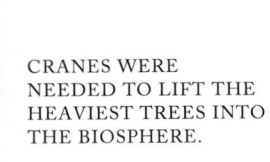

CRANES WERE
NEEDED TO LIFT THE
HEAVIEST TREES INTO
THE BIOSPHERE.

as high as 20 feet tall — from the greenhouses to the rainforest. As the trees arrived by forklift, they seemed to literally fly through the air to their new home. At the same time, plants were being brought in for the other biomes, the ocean's coral reef was being stocked, and the spaceframe roof was still under construction. This was one of Biosphere 2's busiest times!

After the tree-planting phase, smaller plants were added. The mountain's plant pockets proved to be a challenge. They were built to be very deep, so that nutrients could go way down to the bottom. However, the soil kept settling, taking with it the sinking plants! One lesson the planners learned was to make much shallower pockets in future biosphere mountains.

For a dazzling array of surprises and

an inexhaustible fund of enigmas,

there is no part of the world to

compare with a tropical forest. In

South America I have watched what I

thought was a tree trunk turn into a

tapir and walk away.

Gerald Durrell, *A Practical Guide for the Amateur Naturalist*

TAPIR

BAMBOO, BUSHBABIES, AND BUGS

MORPHO
BUTTERFLY

Everyone had a wishlist of plants and animals they wanted to include. The ecologists deliberately packed the Biosphere with many species that could do the same function, because they anticipated a fairly high extinction rate. (As it turned out, their survival rate has been higher than expected.)

Biosphere 2's rainforest owes its start to plants gathered from the countries of Venezuela and Guyana in South America and the Caribbean island of Puerto Rico.

Some seeds and grasses came from Australia, and some plants were shipped to the site from botanical gardens in the United States. The Missouri Botanical Garden was remodeling its rainforest dome (called the Climatron) and lacked the space for some of their larger tropical trees, so its director offered them to Biosphere 2. This generous gift gave the project the boost of more mature specimens.

To make the rainforest as close to

A SNAIL MAKES ITS SLOW WAY ACROSS A BROMELIAD FLOWER.

THE UNDERSTORY OF THE BIOSPHERE 2 RAINFOREST (LEFT) AND THE UNDERSTORY

nature as possible, a wealth of epiphytes, including mosses, orchids, and bromeliads, grace the top of the mountain. Orchids, trees, and vines grow down its side to form a canopy. Staghorn ferns, named for their layers of fronds in the shape of deer horns, are found here. So, too, are bird's nest ferns and other smaller ferns — all epiphytes. Some of these ferns may look familiar to you, because they are commonly used as house plants.

The rainforest's towering canopy includes mango, rubber, and **kapok** (KAY-poc) trees. The sapodilla (SA-poe-DEE-ya) tree is also found here. Its milky juice, known as chicle (CHIC-lay), is the chief ingredient in our chewing gum and accounts for its nickname of 'the chewing gum tree'!

Dr. Ghillean Prance's design strategy was to use these fast-growing tropical trees to filter sunlight falling on the light-sensitive trees of the understory. In Biosphere 2, understory trees include oil palms, guava (GWA-vah), and horseradish trees. The latter got its name from its root, which tastes like horseradish. Many kinds of fruits, fragrant spices, and flowers well adapted to fog, rain, and soggy soil have also been planted here. Adding to the beauty of the rainforest is the passion vine. Its yellow and purple flowers give off a sweet perfume, while its fruit makes a great treat. Many shrubs at this level have

GLIDING FROG

OF THE PUERTO RICAN RAINFOREST (RIGHT) ARE DIFFICULT TO TELL APART.

Colossus of the Tropics

The tallest tree in the Biosphere 2 rainforest is the kapok, also called the ceiba or silk-cotton tree. The kapok grows naturally in southern Asia and tropical America. Its fruit, pollinated by bats, contains seedpods with soft, silky hairs. Before the invention of artificial fibers, these hairs were used as a stuffing for mattresses and life preservers. The oil from its seed is used in cooking, as fuel for lamps, in making soaps, paints, and in cattle feed. Its seed can be roasted and eaten. While it stands, the kapok is home to many animals and plants — a wildlife community as diverse as the boa, the bee, and the jaguar. When cut, its light soft wood can be used for canoes and rafts.

CACAO BEAN

strong medicinal value, including the Madagascar rosy periwinkle. This wonderful plant produces a chemical called vincristine (vin-CHRIS-tin), which is helpful in treating several types of cancer, including lymphatic cancer and childhood leukemia. It had long been used by natives in the Caribbean to treat diabetes, but only recently have scientists realized its value in treating cancer.

Another medicinal plant is the castor oil bean, from which we get castor oil. More to everyone's taste, no doubt, are cacao trees, the source of chocolate. The first crew inside Biosphere 2 had no chocolate treats, because it takes several years for cacao trees to bear fruit. At their first Thanksgiving feast, however, the Mission One biospherians did enjoy a

special treat: coffee brewed with beans picked from a dwarf coffee tree in the rainforest.

Fragrant vanilla and multicolored orchids are some of the epiphytes in the

A VENEZUELAN GUIDE
CUTS A PATH AROUND
A KAPOK TREE.

understory's hanging garden. But the frogs at this level are probably most fond of the bromeliads whose stiff leaves catch rainwater. These natural basins are the perfect spots for the frogs to lay their eggs. Tree ferns, mosses, and lichens add even more variety to the maturing vegetation of the Biosphere's understory, just as in the wild.

VANILLA BEAN

Papaya (pah-PI-yah) trees grow on the north and west sides of the mountain. Peach palms and sugar palms are planted here, too. The peach palms can soar to 60 feet in height and bear clusters of nut-like fruits that are rich in protein. Someday the sugar palms may supply biospherians with sugar palm wine and fibers for caulking or making filters. Below the palms grow Panama hat plants. In Central America, people use their fibers to make hats, ropes, baskets, mats, and brooms. Ceiba and rubber trees also grow here. But, as yet, the crews haven't 'tapped' the rubber trees for their **latex** (LAY-tex) sap.

Further down on the ground level, the helmeted turtles and the garter snakes wander mainly through leaf litter, but there are also short plants, including some gingers, pothos (POE-thos, a viney houseplant), bromeliads, and philodendrons (PHIL-o-DEN-drons). Here, too, earthworms burrow, termites feed on decaying leaves, and other insects keep busy almost everywhere you look. These include fourteen species of ants (not including the stowaways), five species of cockroaches (four selected and one stowaway), and pillbugs.

A sunny 'ginger belt' stands at the foot of the mountain. It's named for its banana plants and other species belonging to the ginger family. These mostly large-leafed plants — in fact, some natives use banana leaves as roofing — were another part of Dr. Prance's plan in building a rainforest. They were planted to shade the interior plants from the sidelight, which can be very harsh in Arizona in the summer. They serve an aesthetic purpose as well, for the ginger belt's array of colorful

HELMETED TURTLE

flowers delight the eyes as well as delight the nose.

A row of bamboo — the giant of the grass family — was planted south of the rainforest to shield it from the ocean's salty sprays. Recent tests to see if there is salt in the rainforest air, however, have proven negative. When the two bamboo species (from the forests of Taiwan and India) are mature they can be used to make sturdy canes, pipes, and poles.

Aside from its natural environment, the rainforest has a technological one. Although the rainforest's canopy has grown thick enough to hide the spaceframes, you can still see sensing devices on the ground level. These sensors take readings every ten seconds on temperature, humidity, rainfall, carbon dioxide levels, and more. For routine monitoring, the Mission Control computers collect about four readings an hour. But should some problem demand a closer look, the ten-second readings can be quickly called up for review.

BAMBOO

The Rainforest's Extra Limbs

Many rainforest trees have thick, rigid growths that extend between their trunk and roots. These woody 'extra legs', known as **buttresses**, provide the extra support needed by the trees because their roots are so near the surface, rather than anchored deep in the ground.

A BANYAN TREE IN A RAINFOREST IN INDIA

What if you, too, were creating a rainforest in a closed environment? What animals would you take in? As you can imagine, the planners of Biosphere 2 had favorites they would have liked to include inside. But only those animals with special characteristics could join the mission. In most cases, each animal had to contribute to the food web system, not weigh or eat too much, and not be too difficult to care for within the confines of Biosphere 2. In the rainforest, this criteria left out such intriguing possibilities as giant armadillos (too big), many of the monkeys (they eat too much), and a hive of honey bees (they require too much care). Dangerous or endangered animals and plants were not considered either. As in the other biomes, most of the rainforest's plants and animals had to be small.

The planners also wanted species that would be comfortable in an environment with high temperature and humidity. After much thought, only one mammal was selected for the 'wild zone'. This is the galago (GAL-ah-go) or bushbaby, a squirrel-sized nocturnal little fellow which won out over other small primates, such as lemurs and monkeys. The planners had wanted a primate because they thought that it would make a good companion for the human crew. Although it did not fill a particular **econiche** (EE-co-nitch), or place in the ecosystem, the biospherians felt it would satisfy their own psychological need for another mammal around. These wide-eyed, nocturnal little creatures would be the closest the biospherians could get to pets like dogs and cats. Native to African rainforests as well as savannahs, galagos enjoy leaping through the tree canopies and vines. Once the galagos got familiar with their wilderness environment, they were expected to have many foods to choose from, since they are omnivores and eat everything from insects and birds to gums and fruits.

Other factors in the galagos' favor were that these cute animals aren't endangered or threatened and are fairly easy to get. Once the decision was made to support four individuals, many decisions about the design of the rainforest took them into account. Additional fig, mango, and

POISON TREE FROGS

banana trees were planted to feed them, and extra food was taken in for them as a safety measure. The three original galagos, Opal, Oxide, and Topaz, had been raised in a laboratory at Duke University and needed time to adjust to getting their own food in the wilderness.

Aside from the galagos, the other mammals chosen for Biosphere 2 were the pigs and goats raised in the farm area.

The initial design of the rainforest allowed for one pair of hummingbirds, two pairs of finches, several species of frogs, lizards, turtles, and snakes. As in nature, the rainforest in Biosphere 2 was stocked with more insects than any other animal. Termites, millipedes, ants, pill bugs, cockroaches, butterflies, and bees were collected from around the world.

BANANA TREES

Collecting in the field was often an adventure, filled with unexpected discoveries. Botanist Linda Leigh recalls one special lesson learned during an expedition in Venezuela. She and her companions were having trouble getting a rope up in a tree so that they could climb up into the canopy. One of their guides, a Yanomamo who lived in the region, laughed and laughed at them. Finally he took their rope, attached it to an arrow, and shot it up over the limb of the tree. His action was as much second nature for him as buckling a seat belt is for us.

RESEARCHERS COLLECT SPECIMENS FOR BIOSPHERE 2 ALONG THE ORINOCO RIVER.

UNDER
WATCHFUL EYES

The biospherians' spirits were high as they began their two-year mission. They were ready to take this historic step into a new world and to study every inch of every biome in Biosphere 2, including its remarkable rainforest.

The person who probably knew the emerging rainforest best was botanist Linda Leigh. As one of her many tasks, she kept a journal of her daily walks through the wilderness. Linda marked certain plants and checked them each month, looking for symptoms of the health of the biome as a whole. She also documented animal populations, counting them and noting nests, droppings, and frequency of their calls.

Linda was also responsible for taking care of the wilderness animals when they got sick or injured. Before closure, she had to give **antibiotics** to one of the blue-tongue skinks (a type of lizard) who had a tail infection. When the galago Topaz was injured, Linda cleaned her wound and gave her antibiotics every day until she recovered. Like the other crew members, Linda was truly an important caretaker of this mini-world.

Were you a biospherian, you would have seen the rainforest undergo many changes during its first two years. As mentioned earlier, fast-growing canopy species were originally planted so that they would quickly shade other plants. However, the quick growers did so well that the thick canopy began providing too much shade for the understory plants. As a result, canopy plants require frequent pruning. The prunings are recycled as food for the animals in the farm area. And in return, **compost** from the farm is used to fertilize the rainforest. Since the last

MARK NELSON AND LINDA LEIGH, MISSION-ONE BIOSPHERIANS, MEASURE TREE GROWTH.

THRASHER

THE GALAGOS CLIMB HIGH UP INTO THE TREES TO EAT ONE OF THEIR FAVORITE FOODS — BANANAS.

two winters in southern Arizona have been cloudier than normal, more shade-loving species have been planted. All these challenges are an important part of the experiment, as researchers learn to assist their special world in adapting to changing conditions.

One of the plants that got out of hand was the morning glory. This vine was originally planted in the mountain's planter pockets. Yet much to everyone's dismay, the plant grew so rapidly that it became a weed, spreading out all over two sides of the mountain. Left unchecked, there would have soon been no room for any other species. In order to preserve the diversity of the area, the biospherians had to remove all of the morning glories. It is interesting how a lovely vine in one place can turn into an unwelcome weed in another by becoming too abundant and threatening diversity.

Many changes have taken place among the animals, too. For instance, the only birds remaining in Biosphere 2 are stowaways. The galagos may have eaten the missing hummingbirds, since Topaz was found high up in the hummingbirds' cage, which had a hole in its screening and no hummingbirds inside. The two cordon bleu finches apparently died from draft problems with the climate-control system. The hummingbirds and finches had been caged, so they wouldn't get snared in nets set up to catch two English sparrows and a curve-billed thrasher that flew in before

closure. Because the thrasher is a songbird, it is protected by law by the U.S. Fish & Wildlife Service. After closure, the biospherians had to get a permit to keep the stowaway inside legally!

The galagos are not really pets that can be 'petted'; they are not tamed. But although they are normally shy, they do sometimes come to the windows between the dining room and the wilderness and peer in at the humans. They have had their share of adventures in the Biosphere, including fights between the two females, Topaz and Opal. As a result of one fight, Opal's wounds required stitches and daily medical care. After a galagologist (a galago specialist) was consulted, Opal was placed in a safe cage for the duration of the first mission.

There was also a galago birth early in the first mission. Linda Leigh was the first to spot the new baby. She reported, "I was up in the hummingbird cage hand feeding the hummingbirds, and I could smell a galago near me. I looked over and there was Topaz with a tiny baby! It was tucked way up into a banana tree about 30 feet off the ground. We didn't know Topaz was pregnant, because galagos are mostly active at night high up in the trees so you rarely see them close up." For that same reason, it is still not known if the first baby born in Biosphere 2's rainforest is a male or female! Linda and the others nicknamed the new addition 'Longtail'.

Both Predators and Protectors

Keystone predators: The major animals that prey on other animals and thus help to control their populations and maintain a balance in the ecosystem.

The biospherians play a double role in the rainforest, as both keystone predators and protectors. Crew members frequently have to climb way up on the spaceframe, belt themselves in like mountain climbers, and cut the overgrown vines which prevent the light from getting down to the plants below. In one sense, the biospherians are acting as predators of the fast-growing plants; but they are also protecting other plants by making sure they get enough sunlight.

Insects Welcome Here

Insects are very important to Biosphere 2. Some are involved in **symbiotic** relationships, helping other plants and animals to survive, such as butterflies and bees that enable plants to reproduce by distributing their pollen. During the maiden voyage of Biosphere 2, the two species of butterflies 'on board' apparently did not reproduce and died out. Butterflies are tricky to raise because they have to be fed throughout both parts of their life cycle, the caterpillar and the adult stage. Often both stages eat different things.

Other rainforest insects, such as termites, are important because they aid in the recycling process. They chew up dead leaves and wood material into smaller elements that then pass into the soil to be reused by the plants.

QUEEN LARVAE CATERPILLARS

Like the birds, the pollinators have also had problems. Butterflies, hummingbirds, and bees were the original pollinators and were expected to service some five hundred plant species in Biosphere 2 that can't reproduce without being pollinated. You know what probably happened to the poor hummingbirds. Unfortunately there are no more bees or butterflies either. Very likely, they perished during the dark winter due to the limited supply of flower nectar for them to eat. But as the plants mature, there will be more and more flowers to support pollinators in the future.

The transition periods between missions offer the chance to repopulate lost species and adjust others as necessary. New populations of pollinators may be brought in, along with other new species. Each new crew has the chance to put to use the findings and lessons of every crew that went before it. In a way, we do the same in the global biosphere — each new generation benefiting from what's been learned before.

Breath of the Rainforest

The project as a whole has had many challenges to meet at every phase. The construction of Biosphere 2 — including the problem of how to seal the structure so that no air got in or out of it — and the installation of all the microbes, plants, and animals was just the beginning! Every day has brought new challenges, new discoveries. But since closure, the most serious challenges have been the excess of carbon dioxide, the drop in oxygen, and fewer crops than expected on the farm.

During their first winter, carbon dioxide levels rose to nearly 10 times the levels in Earth's atmosphere, probably due to the slow plant growth caused by the unusually cloudy weather. While the excess carbon dioxide did not endanger the crew, it was a possible health risk to the ocean's plants and

animals. So a mechanical carbon dioxide 'recycler' that swallows up carbon dioxide from the air helped reduce the excess. When the days grew longer and sunlight increased, the carbon dioxide started to drop and the recycler was turned off.

The crew also alters the 'seasons' in the savannah and the desert so that more plants are active in the winter when the carbon dioxide level is high. The rainforest plays its role in Biosphere 2 just as in Biosphere 1 by year-round absorption of carbon dioxide.

As mentioned earlier, scientists world-wide are not sure about what an increase of carbon dioxide in Earth's atmosphere will do to our global climate. Because Biosphere 2 is such a long-term experiment, it may help show just what the lasting effects of change in the amount of this very important gas might be.

Another challenge was the mysterious loss of oxygen inside the Biosphere. When the first mission began, the oxygen level was 21%, the same as the air the rest of us breathe at low altitudes. But after a year and a half, the oxygen level had dropped

THE LUSH BIOSPHERE 2 RAINFOREST OVERLOOKS THE MINIATURE OCEAN.

to 14%, roughly equivalent the air at the top of a 13,000-foot mountain. Although the plants seemed to suffer no ill effects, the decline in oxygen began to cause some health problems, including fatigue, shortness of breath, headaches, and loss of appetite.

According to some experts, if the oxygen level continued to fall, it could

have hit 13% by the end of the mission. That's equivalent to the thin air on top of an 18,000-foot mountain. Below that, permanent brain damage might occur! Since the cause of the oxygen loss could not be found and stopped, oxygen had to be pumped into the Biosphere to bring it up to 19%. Soon after, the symptoms of oxygen deficiency disappeared.

Since Biosphere 2 is a closed system and every bit of air that escapes is monitored and measured, scientists knew that the missing oxygen was still

somewhere inside. They now know that oxygen is reacting with the rich organic soil in the Biosphere to form carbon dioxide. The newly formed carbon dioxide then sinks into the concrete lining and supports of the huge Biosphere 2 basement. What consequences this holds for Biosphere 2 (and what this may mean to Biosphere 1, as well) remain to be seen as the experiment continues.

As this unique experiment evolves, all of the wilderness biomes remain in excellent condition. The rainforest grows richer and greener every day. One of the trees that visitors see hugging the glass is the *Leuceana*, considered fast-growing because it springs up twelve feet a year. The ones in Biosphere 2's rainforest have been increasing twenty feet a year! Judging by growth rate and abundance, the plants in general seem to have found a perfect home in Biosphere 2.

Looking back, Linda Leigh thinks of the first crew as builders of the basic framework of this amazing laboratory. Each crew that follows then adds to it.

There is still — and always will be — much data to gather about the Biosphere 2 rainforest. Scientists continue to study its function as part of the entire Biosphere. Just as important, they want to know what plants and animals work best in this type of closed system. Among the key items on their agenda is learning the details of the rainforest food web. They also want to explore how natural events inside Biosphere 2 — such as the timing of flowering and fruiting — might differ from those same events on the outside. But it may be quite awhile before they reach any conclusions. As scientists, they realize that perseverance and discipline are needed. For now, they are busy collecting as much data as possible about the complex inner workings of the rainforest along with the other biomes.

BULLFROG

MEANWHILE ... ON THE OUTSIDE

Even as the crews in Biosphere 2 diligently record data and share findings with scientists on the outside, Biosphere 1's rainforests continue to disappear. Some experts estimate that at the current rate of destruction, as many as one hundred species a day vanish forever!

Among the rainforests' worst enemies are loggers who cut down its most profitable trees to sell and unintentionally destroy many other plants as well. Downed trees may take with them many species that exist nowhere else on Earth, including those from which wonder drugs might come someday.

The roads that loggers build in the rainforests also bring more outsiders, including landless farmers. Poor farmers in countries such as Brazil and Venezuela are forced to take whatever land they can get because the best land is controlled by big companies that raise crops (such as coffee and cocoa) for

FERNS GROW ALMOST EVERYWHERE IN A RAINFOREST.

export. The poor farmers cut down the forest, burn the undergrowth, and then soon exhaust the thin rainforest soil. Often they will abandon their plots for new ones, leaving behind barren stretches of rainforest at the mercy of erosion.

Cattle ranchers pose another threat as they clear and burn the rainforest for grazing land on which to raise beef cattle. The last hamburger you ate at a fast food restaurant may have come from cattle

A SECTION OF THE AMAZON RAINFOREST BEING BURNED TO MAKE ROOM FOR CATTLE.

situation may seem to us, we only see part of the total picture. The unseen tragedy is the loss of thousands of rainforest plants and animals yet unknown to us.

So it is with good reason that William Beebe, a famous naturalist, called the forest canopy "an undiscovered continent." Until very recently, scientists often could not study the canopy until its trees fell to the ground. Almost all of the many commercial products we use from the rainforest are found on the lower levels. Meanwhile, the most populated part of the rainforest is the canopy!

Today, new methods are opening up this fascinating and hitherto unreachable world. Scientists from the Smithsonian Tropical Research Institute climb to their study site in the forest of Barro Colorado Island, Panama, on a 138-foot tower. Other new methods to explore the canopy include dropping huge inflatable rafts onto the treetops from airships or helicopters, the use of construction cranes, and nailing ladders to trees with walkways suspended between them.

Around the world, these innovations help scientists to make new discoveries practically every day. New species — especially of insects — are often found in any newly studied patch of rainforest. Even novice scientists enjoy the thrill of discovery here within a short time.

raised on land that was once a rainforest! Also to blame are government officials who authorize the construction of highways in the rainforests or hydro-electric plants damming their rivers.

Finally, there are the miners seeking gold, diamonds, tin, and other minerals. In the Amazon, miners dump mercury and other **toxins** used to process the gold into streams, killing the fish and ruining the drinking water. As serious as the

Those who care about the rainforest are trying to save it in several ways. In some places, conservationists, ecologists, and other scientists have established national parks and reserves for vital rainforests.

One such park is the Ranonafana National Park on the island of Madagascar off the southeast coast of Africa. Established by an American professor, the park helps provide schools, clinics, and technical support for fishermen and farmers in the area. It also protects endangered species of lemurs, the most ancient of primates alive today.

Another kind of conservation effort is the biosphere reserve, a concept developed by the United Nations. Biosphere reserves are chosen for their genetic importance, rather than their scenic splendor. They are divided into various zones, each with its own regulations. The core zone in the middle is the most protected section, while the other surrounding zones all contribute to the protection of the core. Today, one quarter of the 250 biosphere reserves in 65 countries protect tropical rainforests, such as the Lancandon Forest in Mexico.

Rainforests are also being protected from within by the people who live there. The Kuna (ka-OO-na) Indians, a tribe of fifty thousand people who live on islands along the coast of Panama, have turned a large part of their tribal territory into a nature reserve. Kuna Park, the first in the world created by a native group, is supported by funds from tourists and visiting scientists.

However, saving the rainforests does not have to mean barring outsiders. It can mean 'ecotourism', where people travel not only for their own amusement but to learn about the environmental needs of a particular area. It can also mean using the rainforests wisely, so that their natural resources renew themselves. Some loggers are starting to use improved methods to cut down the trees they want without damaging those beside them. Techniques are also being developed for farmers to raise crops that won't harm the rainforest. And scientists are becoming better at analyzing which government projects could endanger the rainforest and then suggesting other locations.

In June 1992, the leaders of many nations met in Brazil to discuss ways to protect the world's environment. Several agreements were drawn up to encourage all people to fight pollution, toxic waste, and rainforest destruction, among other problems. Three hundred thousand youngsters pledged their help!

LEMUR

But the rainforest needs more than our protection. Its mysteries are in great need of exploration and examination by scientists of all kinds. These include environmentalists and ecologists, ethnobotanists, herpetologists, biologists, microbiologists, and entomologists. The more we know about rainforest plants and animals, the better able we are to appreciate their value and to use them wisely.

Biosphere 2 crew member Mark Nelson often thought about the rainforest's importance, not only to Earth's future but also to our exploration of the solar system and beyond. When we eventually take off toward the stars, he hopes to see some of the unique beauty of the rainforests go with us.

"When we think about going into space, we certainly have to start modestly," he says. "But can you imagine living an entire life without enjoying all the incredible little things that happen in a natural ecosystem such as a rainforest? Like the sense of wonder you get when a plant that you've been watching for three months suddenly decides to put out its flower. It's hard to imagine a world where you don't have that kind of mystery and beauty around you."

The mystery and beauty of Earth's rainforests, as well as their necessity, are becoming clearer every day.

Design by Kimura-Bingham Design
Art direction by Linnea Gentry · Illustrations by David Fischer
Engravings from public archival sources

Photographs: Pages 4-5, Tom Lamb. Page 5, D. P. Snyder. Page 7, Matt Finn. Page 9, Matt Finn. Page 13, top, Robert Hahn; bottom, Matt Finn. Page 15, Carol Gracie. Page 16, top and bottom, Carol Gracie. Page 18, Linnea Gentry. Page 20, Matt Finn. Pages 20-21, Matt Finn. Page 21, bottom left, Robert Hahn; bottom right, Margaret Collins. Page 22, Matt Finn. Page 24, Matt Finn. Page 25, Carol Gracie. Pages 26-27, Matt Finn. Page 27, Robert Hahn. Page 28, courtesy of NASA. Pages 30-31, Ghillean Prance. Page 31, middle, Harry Scott; top, Ghillean Prance. Page 35, Scott McMullen. Page 36, frog, C. Allan Morgan. Pages 36-37, C. Allan Morgan. Page 38, Mark Nelson. Page 39, left, Gill Kenny; top right, Harry Scott; bottom right, A. Henderson. Page 40, C. Allan Morgan. Pages 40-41, C. Allan Morgan. Page 41, Jeff Topping. Page 42, D. P. Snyder. Pages 42-43, C. Allan Morgan. Page 44, snail, Matt Finn; right, Matt Finn. Page 45, left, C. Allan Morgan; frog, D. P. Snyder Page 46, Harry Scott. Page 49, Mary Evans. Page 50, Harry Scott. Page 51, Abigail Alling. Page 52, Gill Kenny. Page 54, Steve Prchal. Page 56, C. Allan Morgan. Pages 58-59, Matt Finn. Page 59, Carol Gracie.

GLOSSARY

algae: the simplest forms of green organisms, such as the green scum that forms on the sides of swimming pools.

antibiotic: a substance that destroys or weakens harmful bacteria.

bacteria: a large group of single-celled microscopic organisms which live in water, soil, or the bodies of plants and animals.

biology: the science that studies all forms of life.

biome: a distinct natural region where plants, animals, and other organisms live under similar conditions of climate, terrain, and altitude.

biosphere: the domain of life, the part of Earth in which life exists or which can support life, made up of many complex ecosystems.

botany: the branch of biology that studies plants.

bromeliads: a group of plants with stiff leaves that usually grow attached to trees and cliffs.

buttress: the extra-broad trunk base that helps keep many rainforest trees from falling.

canopy: the top layer of the rainforest, consisting of interconnected tree crowns.

carnivore: an animal that eats other animals for food.

compost: a mixture of decaying organic matter that is used as fertilizer.

convection: the movement of air whereby hot air rises and cold air sinks.

decomposition: the breaking down of dead plant or animal matter that returns nutrients to the soil.

detritivore: an animal that eats decomposing matter.

diversity: a wide variety of forms.

ecology: the branch of biology that studies the balance and interrelationship of living things and their environment.

econiche: the place and function of an organism within its ecosystem.

ecosystem: a community of living things and their environment which together form a functioning unit.

emergent: a rainforest tree that rises above the surrounding forest canopy.

entomologist: a scientist who studies insects.

epiphyte: a plant that gets its nutrients from air and water rather than from soil. Epiphytes often grow on trees.

Equator: an imaginary circle that lies halfway between Earth's North and South poles and divides the planet into the Northern Hemisphere and the Southern Hemisphere.

erosion: the wearing away of soil by the action of ice, water, and wind.

ethnobotanist: a scientist who studies the use of plants by tribal peoples.

evaporate: to change from a liquid to a gas.

extinct: completely died out; having no members of a species left.

fodder: feed for livestock, often made by mixing coarsely chopped stalks and leaves with hay.

food web: the complex cycle of food, food eaters, and waste matter.

fossil fuels: fuels formed underground from the compression of dead plant and animal matter.

fungi: a large group of simple organisms that lack chlorophyll, including molds, mildews, and mushrooms.

gene: a combination of organic molecules in living things that contain the instructions for reproduction.

greenhouse effect: rise in world temperature caused by an increase of carbon dioxide and other gases that trap heat in the atmosphere.

habitat: the place within an ecosystem where an organism naturally lives and grows.

herbivore: an animal that eats only plants.

herpetologist: a scientist who studies reptiles and amphibians.

kapok: a giant rainforest tree with many uses.

keystone predators: the most important animals that prey on other animals and thus help to control their populations.

latex: the milky sap of certain plants, used to make such things as rubber and chewing gum.

lichen: a plant made up of algae and fungi, in a mutually beneficial relationship, that usually grows on hard surfaces.

microbe: a tiny organism, such as bacteria, that can only be seen under a microscope. (Synonymous with **microorganism**.)

microbiologist: a scientist who studies microbes and their effect on other forms of life.

nocturnal: active mostly at night.

omnivore: an animal that eats both plants and other animals.

orchids: a group of flowering epiphytes that contains more species (about 20,000) than any other plant family on Earth.

pesticide: a substance used to kill insects and other animals which are considered pests.

photosynthesis: the process by which plants use energy from the sun to make their food from water, carbon dioxide, and minerals.

pollen: a powderlike substance, produced by flowering plants, that contains male reproductive cells.

pollutant: a substance that harms the environment.

primate: any animal of the order Primates, which includes monkeys, apes, and humans.

respiration: the process by which living things take in oxygen and release carbon dioxide.

species: a group of closely related living things that are able to breed with each other.

symbiosis: a relationship developed for the mutual benefit of two or more individuals.

temperate zone: the climate zone between the tropics and the arctic.

toxin: a poisonous substance.

transpiration: the release of water vapor from plant leaves.

tropics: the area flanking the Equator usually associated with year-round warm weather and high rainfall.

understory: the level of the rainforest between the canopy and the forest floor.

zoology: the branch of biology that studies animals.

FOR FURTHER READING

Aldis, Rodney. *Ecology Watch Rainforests*. New York: Dillon Press, 1991.

Attenborough, David, Philip Whitfield, Peter D. Moore, and Barry Cox. *The Atlas of the Living World*. Boston: Houghton Mifflin Co., 1989.

Dorros, Arthur. *Rainforest Secrets*. New York: Scholastic, 1990.

Durrell, Gerald. *A Practical Guide for the Amateur Naturalist*. New York: Alfred A. Knopf, Inc., 1983.

Durrell, Lee. *State of the Ark*. New York: Doubleday & Co., 1986.

Eyewitness Handbook of Butterflies and Moths. New York: Dorling Kindersley, 1992.

Eyewitness Science: Ecology. New York: Dorling Kindersley, 1991.

Gentry, Linnea and Karen Liptak. *The Glass Ark: The Story of Biosphere 2*. New York: Viking/Puffin, 1991.

George, Jean Craighead. *One Day in the Tropical Rain Forest*. New York: Thomas Y. Crowell, 1990.

Goodman, Billy. *The Rain Forest*. New York: Tern Enterprise, 1991.

Matthews, Rupert. *Explorer*. New York: Eyewitness Books/Alfred A. Knopf, 1991.

Nation, James. *Tropical Rainforests' Endangered Environment*. New York: Franklin Watts, 1988.

Schreider, Helen and Frank. *Exploring the Amazon*. Washington, D.C.: National Geographic Society, 1970.

INDEX

Page numbers in italic (slanted) type refer to pictures.